Our TEXAS

Jackie Mims Hopkins

Illustrated by Craig J. Spearing

Charlesbridge

For my long, tall, Texan brother, Kerry
—J. M. H.

For Dar: Renaissance man, geologist,
park ranger, and a great dad
—C. J. S.

Published by Charlesbridge
85 Main Street
Watertown, MA 02472
(617) 926-0329
www.charlesbridge.com

Library of Congress Cataloging-in-Publication Data
Hopkins, Jackie.
    Our Texas / Jackie Hopkins ; Illustrated by Craig J. Spearing.
        p. cm.
    ISBN 978-1-57091-725-7 (reinforced for library use)
    ISBN 978-1-57091-726-4 (softcover)
1. Texas—Description and travel—Juvenile literature. I. Spearing,
Craig, ill. II. Title.
F386.3.H659 2009
917.64'04—dc22   2009004305

Printed in Singapore
(hc) 10 9 8 7 6 5 4 3 2 1
(sc) 10 9 8 7 6 5 4 3 2 1

Illustrations done in colored pencil on Canson paper
Display type and text type set in Saddlebag and Stone Serif
Color separations by Chroma Graphics, Singapore
Printed and bound September 2009 by Imago in Singapore
Production supervision by Brian G. Walker
Designed by Diane M. Earley

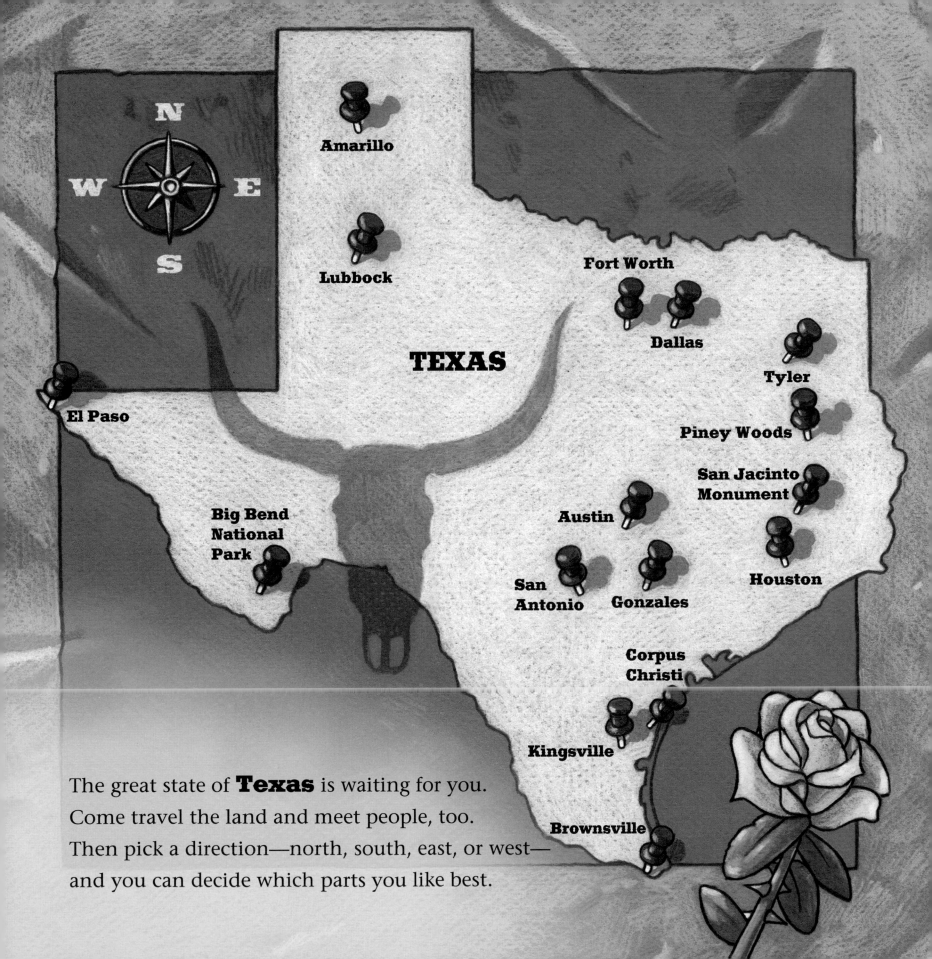

The great state of **Texas** is waiting for you.
Come travel the land and meet people, too.
Then pick a direction—north, south, east, or west—
and you can decide which parts you like best.

Head south to the Valley, where citrus is grown.

The Ruby Red grapefruit is very well known.

The next stop is **Brownsville**, where veggies abound.

There's plenty of sunshine, so crops grow year-round.

In **Kingsville** you'll find a huge, cattle-filled spread:
the King Ranch, where Santa Gertrudis are bred.
It's famous for cowboys. More skilled than ranch hands,
these expert *vaqueros* can ride, rope, and brand.

Corpus Christi was once a frontier trading post
where ships brought in goods to the shops on the coast.
Today you can search for some whelks by the bay
or tour the aquarium: dolphins at play!

Gonzales is where many Texians cried, "No!"

They wished to escape an unjust Mexico.

Here stands the small cannon they named Come and Take It.

Soldados did try, but they never could make it.

In **Houston** the oil barons crave Texas tea!
That black gold's a priceless commodity.
The city hosts NASA and its astronauts
whom Mission Control oversees from this spot.

Historic **San Jacinto's** a flat coastal plain.
Its battleground rang with a famous refrain.
"Remember the Alamo!" was shouted by all.
Here Sam Houston caused Santa Anna to fall.

SAM HOUSTON

SANTA ANNA

And now to East Texas, with **Piney Woods** tall.
Hush, listen . . . perhaps it's the mockingbird's call.
The Caddo once lived here, and peace was their aim;
they called themselves *tayshas*—our state got its name!

In **Tyler** they grow the great Harison's rose,
Each garden's so sweet, you can follow your nose.
The gardens are lovely; there's so much to see—
just look over there, and you'll find a pecan tree.

O'er yonder is **Dallas**, which some call Big D.
Its shops and its market are right for a spree.
There's wheelin' and dealin' at the Texas state fair.
Big Tex greets the crowds, saying, "Howdy!" with flair.

On the North Central Plains in **Fort Worth** see the sale
of the longhorns that rumble along Chisholm Trail.
Get ready to rodeo—cheers fill the night.
Here cowboys and cowgirls compete with delight.

Up north in the Panhandle sits **Amarillo**.

There are plenty of cattle, but few armadillo.

The Grand Canyon of Texas is something to view.

With luck you might spy the horned toad in there, too.

You're heading to **Lubbock**. Prepare for a show
as prairie dogs pop from their burrows below.
The farmers sow seeds and grow cotton in rows,
employing the West Texas wind as it blows.

Due west in the desert is grand old **El Paso**,
where tumbleweeds whirl through as swift as a lasso.
In colonial times pioneers showed no fear
as they braved this old town on the Wild West frontier.

At **Big Bend** coyotes can prowl in the dark
while hunting their prey in this national park.
Vacationers raft down the wild Rio Grande
or look at the dinosaur bones in the sand.

San Antonio's home to a mission so grand;
at the Alamo many men took their last stand.
The loveliest spot is the fine River Walk—
a great place to dine, take a stroll, or just talk.

In **Austin** the state congress meets to debate
the laws that will govern our great Lone Star State.
The capital's known for its wonderful sights—
like bats from the Congress Ave. bridge taking flight.

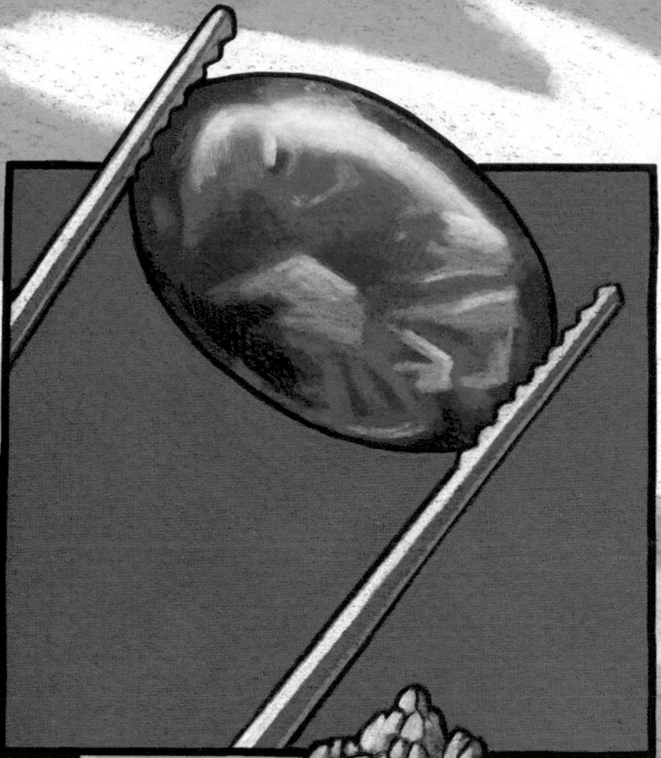

State Gemstone
Blue Topaz

You've seen some of Texas—its splendors galore.
The next time you visit, come see a bunch more.
Our motto is Friendship, and most will agree
that deep in its heart is the best place to be.

State Flower
Bluebonnet

State Animal (small)
Armadillo

State Insect
Monarch Butterfly

State Dish
Texas Chili

State Vegetable and State Pepper
1015 Sweet Onion & Jalapeño

Brownsville

★ In 1846, during the Mexican-American War, the Mexican army attacked Fort Texas. The fort's commander, Major Jacob Brown, was killed. In honor of Major Brown, the post was renamed Fort Brown, and the city of Brownsville developed around it.

★ Brownsville is the southernmost city in Texas. It's also the largest city in the Rio Grande valley.

★ Texans call the area at the southern tip of Texas the Valley, but it's really a flat plain. The Rio Grande flows through it. Early settlers from Mexico called the plain a valley instead of a delta or a floodplain to entice tourists to visit.

★ Due to the warm, mild climate in Brownsville, agriculture is an important part of the area's economy. One of the major crops in the Valley is citrus fruit. In 1993 the Texas legislature designated the Ruby Red grapefruit the official state fruit.

Kingsville

★ Henrietta King, the widow of Captain Richard King, sold part of King Ranch in order to create Kingsville.

★ Established in 1904, Kingsville is in the heart of the world-famous King Ranch. The largest ranch in the United States, King Ranch is larger than the state of Rhode Island.

★ Captain King developed the Santa Gertrudis breed. It was the first recorded strain of cattle created in the Western Hemisphere. This hardy beef cow can weigh almost two thousand pounds.

★ As the ranch grew, Captain King hired many Mexican ranch hands, who became known as *Kineños*, or King's men. The Spanish word for cowboy is *vaquero*.

Corpus Christi

★ Almost five hundred years ago, Alonso Alvarez de Pineda, a Spanish explorer, visited the area now known as Corpus Christi. The city is named after the Roman Catholic feast day that celebrates the body of Christ.

★ Corpus Christi began as a frontier trading post and has developed into the largest city on the Texas coast.

★ The sun shining on the bay causes the water to sparkle, resulting in the city's nickname, Sparkling City by the Sea.

★ Across the water from the Corpus Christi harbor is the Padre Island National Seashore, where the state shell, the lightning whelk, can be found. This shell is named for its colored stripes and is one of the few shells that open on the left side.

Gonzales

★ The first battle of the Texas Revolution took place in Gonzales, one of the earliest Anglo settlements in Texas. Mexican soldiers, called *soldados* in Spanish, came to retrieve a cannon that they had previously loaned to the American colonists, called Texians, to protect them from Indian raids. The soldiers demanded the cannon, and the Texians pointed at it and said, "There it is—come and take it." The settlers had made a flag or banner with a white background and a lone star above a black cannon. The words "come and take it" were written under the cannon. The settlers flew the flag in protest.

★ Each year during the first weekend of October, the town of Gonzales celebrates the first shot of the Texas Revolution with the Come and Take It Festival. The three-day festival includes a reenactment of the battle that occurred near Gonzales during the early-morning hours of October 2, 1835, in which the *soldados* were driven back without retrieving the cannon.

Houston

★ In August 1836 Augustus and John Allen, brothers from New York City, purchased land along Buffalo Bayou with the intent of establishing a city. They named the city after Sam Houston, the hero of the Texas Revolution and the anticipated first president of the new Republic of Texas.

★ Houston is the fourth-largest city in the United States and is home to the world's largest concentration of medical professionals.

★ Lyndon Baines Johnson was one of two U.S. presidents born in Texas. He became the thirty-sixth president in 1963 after the assassination of John F. Kennedy. Among Johnson's many accomplishments was his work on America's space program, a cause he supported from the time he was the senate majority leader in the 1950s.

★ Houston is nicknamed Space City because of NASA's Johnson Space Center. Established in 1961, the center has been responsible for every crewed NASA mission since the launch of *Gemini 4* in 1965. "Houston" was the first word spoken from the surface of the moon in 1969.

San Jacinto Monument

★ The San Jacinto Monument marks the site of the final battle of the Texas Revolution. During the surprise attack led by Sam Houston, the Texians yelled, "Remember the Alamo!" The Texians gained control of the Mexican camp in eighteen minutes.

★ Recognized as a National Historic Civil Engineering Landmark by the American Society of Civil Engineers, the 570-foot San Jacinto Monument is the world's tallest war memorial.

★ The San Jacinto Monument is so huge that there is a museum inside the base of the tower. The star on top of the tower weighs 220 tons!

★ The San Jacinto Battleground State Historic Site is home to the battleship *Texas*. The *Texas* became the first battleship memorial museum in the United States, and it is the only remaining battleship to have served in World War I. The *Texas* is also the only remaining ship that served in both world wars.

Piney Woods

★ Piney Woods, also know as East Texas, is famous for its many species of pine trees. Longleaf, piñon, shortleaf, and loblolly can all be found in the Piney Woods. Several varieties of hardwood trees, such as hickory and oak, also thrive in the area.

★ The Caddo Indians once lived in this wooded region. They hunted in the dense forests and farmed in the clearings. They grew corn, beans, pumpkins, and squash.

★ The word "Texas" comes from a Caddo word meaning "friends." The Caddo Indians called each other *tayshas*, which the Spanish spelled *Tejas* (TAY haws). Mexicans who lived in the Texas Republic were called *Tejanos* (tay-HAN-ohs). The state motto of Texas is Friendship.

★ There are hundreds of species of birds in the Piney Woods, including the mockingbird, the state bird of Texas. This clever bird is able to imitate the sounds made by other birds, crickets, and frogs, and even mechanical sounds like the screeching of car tires.

Tyler

★ Tyler's nickname is the Rose Capital of America because of its role in the rose-growing industry. Roses grown in Tyler and Smith County are shipped to gardeners all over the world.

★ The nation's largest municipal rose garden is located in Tyler and hosts the Texas Rose Festival each October. This fourteen-acre rose garden has close to forty thousand rose bushes, including the famous yellow rose of Texas. The official name of the yellow rose of Texas is Harison's Yellow.

★ The city was named for President John Tyler in recognition of his support for Texas's admission to the United States.

★ The state tree of Texas is the pecan tree. Former Texas governor James Hogg loved the tree so much that he asked for one to be planted near his grave. Pecan nuts from his tree are planted all over Texas in his honor.

Dallas

★ In 1841 John Neely Bryan founded the city of Dallas with a single cabin on the Trinity River.

★ In 1890 Dwight David Eisenhower, the thirty-fourth president, was born in Denison, Texas, which is about 75 miles north of Dallas. He was a World War II hero and served two terms as president of the United States.

★ The Dallas metropolitan area has more shopping centers per capita than any other city in the United States. It also has the Dallas Market Center, the largest wholesale trade complex in the world.

★ Each year Dallas hosts the State Fair of Texas. As visitors enter the fairgrounds, they are welcomed by a "Howdy" from Big Tex. This fifty-two-foot-tall cowboy has a seventy-five-gallon hat and a size seventy pair of boots. One of the favorite attractions at the fair, the Texas Star, is the largest Ferris wheel in the Western Hemisphere.

Fort Worth

★ Fort Worth was one of the many stops along the Chisholm Trail, a famous cattle trail. Millions of head of cattle, including the state's own Texas longhorns, were driven along this trail.

★ In keeping with Fort Worth's nickname, Cowtown, cowhands drive Texas longhorn cattle down Fort Worth's Exchange Avenue every day.

★ Fort Worth's National Cowgirl Museum and Hall of Fame is the only museum in the world solely dedicated to honoring women of the American West.

★ The United States Bureau of Engraving and Printing produces United States paper currency in Fort Worth. The only other city to produce the nation's Federal Reserve notes is Washington, DC.

Amarillo

★ Amarillo's nickname, the Yellow Rose of Texas, may come from the yellow wildflowers that grow in the area or from the nearby yellow soil along the banks of Amarillo Lake and Amarillo Creek. The Spanish word for yellow is *amarillo*, pronounced "am-uh-REE-yoh," but the city of Amarillo is pronounced "am-uh-RIL-oh."

★ Palo Duro Canyon, the second-largest canyon in the United States, is often called the Grand Canyon of Texas. Spanish explorers called the area Palo Duro, which is Spanish for hard wood. Mesquite and juniper trees are some of the hardwood trees found throughout the canyon.

★ Palo Duro Canyon has many species of wildlife, including the rare Texas horned lizard. The Texas horned lizard is the state reptile and was one of the first animals to be listed as a threatened species in Texas.

Lubbock

★ Lubbock is located in one of the oldest inhabited areas in Texas. North of the city, archaeologists have discovered evidence of twelve thousand years of human existence in a canyon called Yellow House Draw. Fossils of mammoths, giant bison, and a giant armadillo have also been found in this area.

★ This area is the largest uninterrupted cotton-growing region in the world and one of the primary centers for cottonseed processing.

★ Prairie Dog Town, in Mackenzie State Park, is a popular Lubbock attraction. Prairie dogs live underground in colonies. These burrowing rodents pop up from their homes and make barking sounds.

★ Lubbock's nickname is Hub City. Lubbock is the educational, economic, and health care hub for the South Plains region.

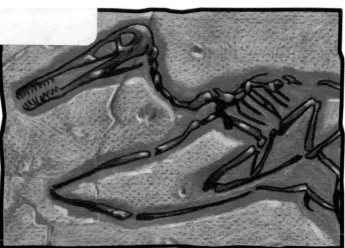

El Paso

★ El Paso is the westernmost city in Texas. It's located among mile-high peaks in the Franklin Mountains. *El paso* is Spanish for "the pass."

★ El Paso is the only Texas city in the Mountain Time Zone; the rest of Texas is in the Central Time Zone.

★ In the Chihuahuan Desert, where the mountains of El Paso are located, tumbleweeds are abundant. When the tumbleweed plant matures and dries out, the wind breaks off the plant at the soil line. The rounded shape of the plant causes the plant to roll and tumble, blown by the West Texas winds.

★ In 1581 Spanish explorers discovered what would one day be El Paso when they saw two mountain ranges with a pass between them. In 1682 the Tigua Indians founded their pueblo, Ysleta del Sur Pueblo, within the city limits of El Paso. Today, they are one of the few Native American groups in Texas.

Big Bend National Park

★ Big Bend National Park is located in West Texas on a gigantic bend of the Rio Grande. One legend explains that after creating Earth, the creator of the world threw all the leftover rocks onto the land of Big Bend.

★ The park is in the Chihuahuan Desert and includes archaeological sites that are nearly ten thousand years old.

★ In 1971 Douglas A. Lawson found the radius bone of a pterodactyl in Big Bend. It was larger than any discovered before. The pterodactyl's wingspread was about forty feet long!

★ At El Paso the Rio Grande forms the international boundary between Mexico and the United States, and it empties into the Gulf of Mexico at Brownsville. The 1,896-mile-long river is the twenty-second-longest in the world and the fourth-longest in the United States. A 196-mile-long strip of the river is called the Rio Grande Wild and Scenic River. The river forms the distinctive big-bend shape of Texas.